CANADA *and the* QUEST FOR PEACE

◪ JACOB BLAUSTEIN LECTURES
IN INTERNATIONAL AFFAIRS

CANADA *and the*
QUEST FOR PEACE

BY PAUL MARTIN

1967

COLUMBIA UNIVERSITY PRESS

NEW YORK & LONDON

PAUL MARTIN is Secretary of State for External Affairs of Canada and Member of Parliament (Essex East).

⚓ FOREWORD

THIS BOOK, *Canada and the Quest for Peace,* by Paul
Martin, Secretary of State for External Affairs, consists
of three chapters, which were presented initially as
lectures in the first series of Jacob Blaustein Lectures
in International Affairs scheduled under the auspices
of the School of International Affairs at Columbia
University. The three chapters, "Canada's Role in
Supporting United Nations Peacekeeping Efforts,"
"Canada's Approach to the Vietnam Conflict," and
"Canada's Contribution to Economic Development
in the Less Developed World," portray three major
contributions of that country to the cause of peace.

In a real sense the story told in these pages requires
no commentary for it portrays with great clarity the
extraordinarily good record of Canada in the quest for
peace in the period since World War II. The story is
accurate and highly informative, and it is at the same
time modestly presented.

During my long tenure at the United Nations I

worked closely with all member nations in peacekeeping and other activities. I have a profound sense of
appreciation for the constructive and statesmanlike
role that Canada always played in efforts to keep the
peace and in sponsoring measures to strengthen the
United Nations. No member nation has had a better
record than Canada in these respects. These excellent
chapters should be read with the recognition of the
extraordinarily fine contribution that Canada has
made to the quest for peace.

On several occasions in this book the author refers
to the Canadian concept of national interest as related
to the policies and programs outlined here. Although
Canada is a middle-sized power, with substantial military strength and material resources, and might well
have interpreted her national interest in terms of traditional policy, she has chosen not to do so. She has
deliberately followed the more enlightened course,
influenced by the nuclear threat to mankind, and has
made the quest for peace inside and outside the
United Nations the central feature of her national
policy. As Mr. Martin states, "It would not be fanciful
to suggest that, having few illusions about the past to
shape our conception of the national interest, we have

tried to frame our policies more fully in terms of future international requirements and responsibilities."

It was a most fortunate development in the fulfillment of United Nations tasks in the field of peacekeeping that the middle-sized and smaller powers were able in part, at least, to fill the void caused by the Cold War. The assumption that the permanent members of the Security Council would work together with sufficient unity to keep the peace never materialized. In fact Cold War elements often intruded into brush fire wars, making it necessary, after Korea, to exclude the great powers from a direct contribution to the quasi-military forces of peacekeeping operations while maximizing the contribution of contingents from the armed forces of the middle-sized and smaller powers. Canada has played a vital role in all United Nations operations of whatever character in the peacerestoring or peacekeeping field, from the Korean war to the present.

Taking into account the numerous problems of peacekeeping operations that have developed since 1961, she has pursued a statesmanlike line of earmarking units of her armed forces and of developing and promoting training programs which are in accord with United Nations principles and projected peace-keeping requirements. At this stage the earmarking of troops, which has been initiated by a number of the members of the United Nations, is far more realistic than the development of a standby force. The rich experience gained from past operations deserves, as the author states, systematic and thorough review, including the development of manuals which should be of great value to the Secretariat, to the governments co-operating in new peacekeeping operations, and to their contingents in the field.

The role of Canada in the Vietnam crisis is conditioned in part by her membership, along with Poland and India, on the International Control Commission, which was set up after the Geneva Conference of 1954. The Commission, although for various reasons lacking in effectiveness, continues to exist and provides something of an entrée to North Vietnam. The Canadian Government, like many other governments, is continuing in its efforts to find a formula for and a means of bringing the war to an end, taking into account particularly the long-range interests of the people of Vietnam.

Mr. Martin suggests a four-stage process of achieving a cease fire, building in part upon the cease-fire provisions of the 1954 settlement. He states that "the war in Vietnam must be brought to an end, and the peaceful future not only of Vietnam but of all South East Asia must be assured. Since 1954 Canada has done its best to prevent a war in Vietnam. It is now doing its utmost to help to bring the war to an end. When a settlement is achieved, we shall do our best to ensure that it is a permanent one."

In Mr. Martin's third lecture he deals with "a different aspect of the search for world peace; namely, the task of international development, and Canada's distinctive contribution to it." Canada in the period since 1950 has contributed liberally to aid programs both inside and outside the United Nations, her per capita contribution being greater than that of the United States.

She has been a major contributor to the Colombo Plan from its beginning and two years ago made an important capital contribution to the new Asian Development Bank. In 1958 Canada extended the scope of her assistance to include the British West Indies and the successor independent states, and in 1960 she began a program of assistance to the Commonwealth African countries. In 1964 Canada engaged in a further extension of her aid program to include new development projects in a number of Central and South American countries working in this connection through the Inter-American Development Bank.

On a wider basis she has, as a member of the Development Assistance Committee of Organization for Economic Cooperation and Development, coordinated her program with the assistance of the other members of the committee to ensure the avoidance of overlapping and to provide maximum assurance of the particular worthiness of selected projects.

Canada has also been a liberal supporter of aid programs sponsored by the United Nations through its Expanded Program of Technical Assistance, its Special Fund, and its current United Nations Development Program. By the early 1970s it is her plan to expand her contribution to international development to an amount approximately equal to one per cent of her Gross National Product, a goal much to be desired but one which will be reached by very few countries by that date.

This series of lectures and others that will follow in succeeding years are made possible by a grant from Mr. Jacob Blaustein, whose interest in international affairs has been amply demonstrated through appointment by five presidents to important missions in the international field and by his membership as alternate representative on the United States Delegation to the General Assembly.

September 1967   ANDREW W. CORDIER
Dean, School of International Affairs at Columbia University

✷ CONTENTS

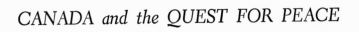
CANADA *and the* QUEST FOR PEACE

◪ CANADA'S ROLE IN SUPPORTING UNITED NATIONS PEACEKEEPING EFFORTS

IT IS APPROPRIATE to begin this series of lectures with the subject of Canada's role in supporting United Nations peacekeeping. Keeping the peace is the primary purpose of the United Nations and is therefore of great significance in itself. I have in mind more especially however that Canada's policies in support of peacekeeping are particularly relevant to an understanding of the Canadian outlook on the world. For reasons which have to do with our geography, our resources, and our relatively recent development as an independent state, we have chosen, perhaps unconsciously, to concentrate a good deal of our foreign policy energies in the realm of international organization. It would not be fanciful to suggest that, having few illusions about the past to shape our conception of the national interest, we have tried to frame our policies more fully in terms of future international requirements and responsibilities. It so happens, as well, that to play our distinctive part in the building of international institutions corresponds to the Canadian urge to look outwards, to find, if we can, a counterweight to the enormous if benign influence of our great neighbor. We have been fortunate moreover to have had some extra margin of wealth and stability to devote to these purposes. If the following discussion suggests that Canada's interests often coincide to a degree that is unusual with the efforts of the United Nations to keep the peace, I shall be well satisfied.

We are accustomed to reading in the press about stalemate, deadlock, or failure at the United Nations on the subject of peacekeeping. These reports are, of course, discouraging. Yet they are also partial. They do not reflect the fact that while there is disagreement in New York there is action in the Middle East, or in Cyprus, or in Africa which helps to preserve the peace. On the one hand, the General Assembly has not been able to reconcile the differences which divide member states over questions of principle, but on the other hand these same member states have responded to clear and urgent requirements to initiate and to keep in being United Nations forces and teams to patrol, to supervise, and to conciliate.

The disagreements are hardly surprising. For the first time in human history something resembling a world community is emerging from the dissolution of empire and the simultaneous spread of technology. Everywhere men pursue the same goals. Yet few are able to measure significant progress in reaching them. Disparities in national wealth, the indignities of racial discrimination, the rivalries stimulated by artificial boundaries and uncertain loyalties—all of these generate tension and conflict on a scale which is worldwide. Yet if the complexities are greater, so is our determination to act together to find solutions.

If we do not act together then the dangers of losing control are all too familiar to our post-Hiroshima generation. Every schoolboy has heard the term "escalation" and knows immediately to what it refers. This too is a new phenomenon. In the past governments have been prepared to go to war if necessary to gain their ends or to defend their interests, knowing that defeat, while never expected, would not destroy the nation state itself. Today no government can take or contemplate military action, whatever the reason, without a strong sense of the limits beyond which all such action would be suicidal.

On the one hand the conditions which make for conflict and the use of armed force in world affairs are of unprecedented scope. On the other hand the potential effects of modern weapons impose on the conduct of states and the calculations of statesmen unprecedented limits. In these circumstances the United Nations is bound to be both a battlefield and a conference room. It must reflect as well as contain the impulse for change. It has served, in the words of one student of the subject, as the registrar of prudential pacifism.

The conditions I have just described were not all foreseen by the founders of the United Nations. Certainly none would have imagined a membership of 122 states after only 22 years. Nor could they have anticipated that one of the major premises of the Charter would prove to be unworkable. This was the assumption that the Permanent Members of the Council would cooperate in order to maintain peace. True, the statesmen of 1945 were not so naive as to expect such cooperation to be automatic. But they did assume that without Great Power understanding the security system laid down in the Charter would not function. The governments which had won the war were quite naturally determined that it should not happen again and that the combined strength of China, France, the United States, the Soviet Union, and the United Kingdom should serve to deter any potential aggressor. If these powers could not agree, it was thought, then no security system could save the peace.

It was not until later that peacekeeping by consent, as we now understand it, and by the lesser powers, came to be regarded as the standard form of United Nations military action. It was this reversal, however, which enabled Canada to participate in peacekeeping in quite unexpected ways. Instead of the Great Powers banding together to threaten any aggressor with overwhelming force, the middle and small powers were called upon to police situations which otherwise might have led to Great Power intervention.

Canada emerged from the Second World War with military capacities and economic strength second only to that of the Great Powers. She had developed close working relationships with the United States and British Governments, and from an early stage was consulted about the postwar institutions and arrangements which were under discussion by these powers. She was aware of a new-found status in world affairs and anxious to enter into commitments which would satisfy this status. Bismarck is said to have once remarked about a European rival that she had developed an appetite for power without the teeth. About Canada it might have been said after the war that she had developed both the appetite and the teeth for a new international role. This was in sharp contrast with Canada's prewar policies which by and large had been directed to avoiding commitments and involvement in the affairs of the world even though she remained a member of the League of Nations.

At San Francisco Canada directed her efforts towards strengthening the provisions of the Dumbarton Oaks proposals in respect of the rights and responsibilities of the so-called middle powers. Canada pressed strongly for the adoption of qualifying rules for election to the Security Council which would recognize the contributions member states might make to the maintenance of international peace and security. This idea was incorporated into Article 23 of the Charter. Canada was also responsible for the adoption of what became Article 44 of the Charter providing for consultation between a member state and the Council before the latter called for the provision of that member's armed forces for enforcement action. The Prime Minister of Canada explained at the time that the imposition of sanctions would "raise especially difficult problems for secondary countries with wide international interests," because while the Great Powers would be able to prevent by the veto any decision to impose sanctions, the so-called secondary countries would apparently not have any choice in the matter, despite the possibility they would be called upon to participate. In addition, Canada was responsible for the provision of the Charter now incorporated in Article 24 (3) which requires the Security Council to report periodically to the General Assembly. The purpose was to give the Assembly some sense of supervision of the Council's acts, although it has not turned out that way. On all these issues Canada pursued policies which were consistent with her wartime record and her postwar position as a leader of the secondary powers.

In subsequent years, Canada continued to look for and to follow policies which satisfied these general capacities and needs. We fully expected to play our proper part in the building of the collective security system sketched in Chapter VII of the Charter and we were alarmed and disappointed by the early signs of disunity in the Security Council and by the breakdown in 1947 of negotiations between the Permanent Members of the Council on the question of United Nations armed forces. We were obliged to turn elsewhere for the satisfaction of our security requirements. Yet even as we ratified the NATO Treaty in 1949 we did not despair of the United Nations' capacity to fulfill its primary purpose. The present Canadian Prime Minister, Mr. Lester Pearson, said in Parliament at the time, for example, that "the North Atlantic Treaty will serve as an instrument which . . . will make it possible for [the free democracies] to use the United Nations with greater confidence and more hope of success."

The United Nations action in Korea was an apparent fulfillment of these hopes. Canada regarded it as the first effective attempt by the United Nations to organize an international force to stop aggression. We had contributed for the first time to the organization's peacekeeping operation when military observers were sent to Kashmir in January 1949. We had also supported the Secretary-General's proposal for a Field Service. But it was not until 1950 and the opportunities provided by the decision to resist aggression in Korea that we began to organize the procedures and to think in the terms which we have followed since.

The Canadian Army Special Force, raised for service in Korea, would, we hoped, have a continuing function in carrying out Canada's obligations under the United Nations Charter. We urged other member states to earmark national contingents so as to be better prepared to resist aggression if and when called upon to do so by the United Nations. We welcomed the establishment by the Assembly of a Collective Measures Committee to look into the details of joint military planning. We appointed a representative to a Panel of Military Experts. Yet once the Korean emergency had passed the United Nations was to hear little more of these bodies. For the members of the NATO Alliance, in particular, the strains and pressures arising from the military build-up in Europe soon pushed into the background the schemes for strengthening the United Nations. Moreover, after 1955 the character of the organization began to change. New member states added their distinctive interests to the torrent of talk and paper. The Western members no longer enjoyed the influence they had been able to bring to bear five years before.

In 1956, however, the development of crisis conditions in the Middle East enabled the United Nations once again to take measures which revived Canada's interest in defining her contribution to collective security. It was the United Nations Emergency Force which was to be the fruitful precedent for the growth of the concept of peacekeeping. For the first time organized military forces were deployed and commanded without participation by the Permanent Members and outside the framework of the cold war. Canada made a special contribution to the ideas behind the new Force as well as providing its first Commander. On the one hand, it was a matter of urgent importance to us that some way should be found to bridge the gap which had opened up between our traditional European allies and the United States. On the other hand, we saw in the situation an opportunity to implement the ideas we had put forward six years before at the time of Korea.

This is not the place to describe the characteristics of peacekeeping forces as they were defined by Mr. Hammarskjöld in the light of the UNEF experience. What I wish to emphasize is that the lesson we drew from our participation in the Force was a further refinement of the earmarking idea. In addition to the desirability of governments themselves earmarking contingents for peacekeeping, we concluded that the Secretariat must be enabled to plan ahead in advance of the next emergency. It was just ten years ago that the present Prime Minister of Canada proposed in an article which appeared in *Foreign Affairs* that governments be invited to signify a willingness to contribute contingents to the United Nations for noncombatant purposes and that some central machinery be created to make advance arrangements and to direct future operations. Since 1957 Canada has herself made arrangements for units of her armed forces to be on standby duty for possible service with the United Nations.

Canada still participated in the Emergency Force ten years after its formation. The nature of our contribution changed as the size of the Force diminished. Yet the circumstances which brought about its dispatch to the Middle East have not appreciably changed. Two questions arise. What have we learned about peacekeeping during these ten years? If the United Nations is to stay in the peacekeeping business, and experience suggests it will, how is responsibility for this task to be shared among the member states?

Let me first try to summarize what we have learned, based not only on our participation in UNEF, but also on our subsequent participation in the Congo Force, the Cyprus Force, and in a number of United Nations Observer Groups sent to patrol frontiers and supervise cease-fires. The first conclusion to be drawn is that each operation is different and that no standard political guidelines will serve to prepare for the next. In the Middle East, for example, we have been called upon to supply a variety of needs including administrative and maintenance support, mobile ground reconnaissance, air reconnaissance, and air transport. In the Congo we were asked to provide signallers. In Cyprus the need was for an infantry battalion. Again the mandates of these various forces and groups have been different, ranging from defensive military action in the Congo to observation and reporting in the Yemen. The observers who went to Lebanon in 1958 did not have the same job as those in the United Nations Truce Supervision Organization who were already stationed on the borders of Israel.

In addition, the composition of each operation has varied with the political and social circumstances. Obviously it is desirable, for example, that troops from African countries should be available for peacekeeping duties in Africa under United Nations auspices. In Cyprus it makes more sense for troops from Western countries, broadly speaking, to be doing the job. On the other hand, the United Nations cannot restrict itself to a regional pattern of composition, for by definition a United Nations force represents the organization as a whole. The Canadian, Scandinavian, and Irish troop contributions to the Congo Force demonstrated that nonregional assistance may be desirable not only for political reasons but for reasons of technical efficiency and experience. I would conclude, therefore, that ad hoc methods of raising forces and some improvisation in planning is an element of contemporary peacekeeping experience which we shall have to accept. This does not mean that planning cannot be done in advance, and I shall make some suggestions in this respect. But we are right to be sceptical of schemes for elaborate staff work and standing forces. We are still at a stage in international military organization where the first priority must be some agreement on the blueprints or master texts of peacekeeping procedures, these to be moulded to fit the individual circumstances of each operation. Even this measure of agreement has proved to be more difficult to accomplish than we expected ten years ago.

I want to emphasize as well the importance of establishing clearly the terms of reference or mandate of a peacekeeping force or observer mission before it is authorized to begin its work. The degree of clarity of such terms of reference will depend to a large extent upon the degree of political consensus which prevails among the parties to the dispute and the other governments concerned. This will usually depend in turn on the nature of the dispute or situation. If the situation involves internal disorder it will be very difficult to lay down a clear-cut mandate. There will be other kinds of situations where the degree of consensus existing in the Council is so fragile that nothing can be agreed other than a general instruction to prevent conflict or to supervise a truce.

It may be that it will be clearly preferable for the United Nations to intervene in these circumstances than for some other organization or government to do so without reference to the United Nations. We may have to accept that the Force Commander and the Secretary-General will have little guidance. However, we should only come to this conclusion, I believe, after having accepted the risk that inadequate terms of reference might do serious harm to the prestige of the United Nations and to its future effectiveness. There will be no easy answers. But the Canadian Government will be bound to give more searching examination to requests for assistance if it is not satisfied that the mandate provides sufficient guidance for the conduct of the troops on the ground.

There is a related point. Even if defined satisfactorily at the beginning of an operation, the mandate may be subject to interpretation or gradual erosion. Freedom of movement, for example, is particularly important for the carrying out of any mission which involves observation of frontiers or the supervision of a return to normal conditions. Generally, it will be in the interest of the parties that such movement be as unrestricted as possible. But there will also be occasions when this is not so. It is now an accepted condition of peacekeeping that the host government consent to the operations and procedures followed by the United Nations. Nor in principle must the United Nations interfere in the internal affairs of the host state. But it must be able to observe, to verify and where necessary to interpose. It will be the more difficult to carry out this task if there is not firm, consistent pressure on the parties to cooperate. Who is to exercise this pressure? It is unfair to expect the Secretary-General to do the job alone. The Security Council must give him the backing he needs. If it cannot do so, then contributors may have no choice but to reexamine their decision to participate in the operation.

A third important conclusion we would draw from our experience is that peacekeeping is a beginning, not an end. Perhaps the day will come when the United Nations is able to provide forces and to maintain bases around the world on a semipermanent basis. But that day has not yet arrived. In the meantime contributions by governments of contingents of their forces for United Nations peacekeeping purposes will be based on the assumption that the parties to the dispute will get on with the job of settling their differences or reestablishing order. The United Nations cannot and must not be responsible for one party clearly gaining the advantage over the other. As a general rule peacekeeping and mediation should proceed concurrently. The Security Council resolution which authorized the Cyprus Force for example also provided for the appointment of a mediator. His report was not acceptable to all the parties to the dispute. But if the latter do not soon find a solution by their own means, then the process of mediation must begin again.

The financing of peacekeeping operations has been a continuing problem, climaxed by the deadlock which prevented the nineteenth session of the Assembly from functioning normally. We have concluded from that experience that collective responsibility for financing, even on the basis of a special assessment scale which would take into account the economic capacities of member states and other relevant considerations, is not a principle which in present circumstances will be enforced by the Assembly. It is naturally in the interests of the countries which contribute contingents to United Nations forces that the costs of these contingents should be equitably shared by all, and there is no doubt in our minds that collective assessment based on a special scale is the most equitable method of meeting peacekeeping costs. It is now apparent, however, that such a method of financing will not be enforceable unless the Security Council so decides. What we would hope is that the Council would in fact decide on this method in most cases. If no agreement can be reached in the Council on that basis then the next most satisfactory method of financing, if conditions permit, is for the parties to the dispute to pay the costs. Voluntary contributions may always be solicited as an extra source of funds where the expenses are heavy and the parties are unable to meet them. But in that case the members of the Council and particularly the Permanent Members should be the first, in my view, to contribute their share. The Permanent Members cannot reasonably claim a preponderant voice in decisions to keep the peace if they will not help finance operations which they have authorized.

The final conclusion I would like to draw from Canadian experience with peacekeeping is that there is a very delicate balance between the requirements for efficiency and neutrality. In general, I would say, the more candidates for peacekeeping the better, even though this may mean some loss of efficiency. Over forty United Nations members have participated in one or more peacekeeping operations. I would hope that this number can be substantially increased. It is disappointing that only a few have informed the United Nations of the kinds of forces or services they might be able to provide if requested to do so. Peacekeeping ought not to be the business of any one group or of those who can best contribute the facilities and services required. Only when United Nations forces represent a wide spectrum of the membership can we be hopeful that the necessary political support will be forthcoming. All member states should be equally eligible, with two qualifications: the Great Powers should not usually be asked to participate nor should states with a direct or particular interest in the dispute or situation. Peacekeeping, after all, is not only a method of preventing or stopping conflict; it is an international experiment from which the peacekeepers themselves have much to learn and which could be a forcing house for international military cooperation with immense long-term benefits for world security.

I have spoken of the past and drawn some conclusions which point to the future. Let me now be more specific about how we might improve the United Nations' capacity to keep the peace. At the last session of the General Assembly Canada cosponsored a Resolution which called for the adoption of a special scale for the financing of peacekeeping operations involving heavy expenditures, and recommended to the Security Council that it authorize a study of the methods of improving preparations for peacekeeping. The resolution also invited member states to communicate information to the United Nations about their own plans and capabilities.

Canada's financing proposals are modest. We accept the fact that where expenditures are more than, say, ten million dollars a year for any one operation, special arrangements must be made to protect the interests of the developing states. We suggest that their share should be fixed at the level of 5 per cent of the total, which is what they paid for UNEF. This would mean that most member states would pay only nominal amounts and then only in cases when the Council recommended this method of financing. Naturally if they agreed to accept a larger share we would be delighted, but we think 5 per cent is a not unreasonable figure. The rest would be divided among the relatively wealthy states, with the Permanent Members paying the major part.

Financial problems were the superficial cause for the stalemate in the Assembly's proceedings of two years ago. Less was heard about the operational aspects of peacekeeping, which have been equally, if not more, controversial. I said earlier that elaborate planning machinery centred in the Secretariat and early agreement on a United Nations permanent force seems unlikely to be realized soon. We strongly believe, nevertheless, that important improvements can be made.

Let me give some examples. Coordinated planning needs to be done on such questions as standard operating procedures, training, logistics, and communications. Model principles might be drawn up for general application in status of forces agreements. The question of comparable standards of pay, leave, and welfare for troops from different countries has not been studied. Governments with peacekeeping experience might consider providing staff courses for the training of officers from other interested countries. A standard training manual needs to be produced. We ought to consider whether at least some standardization of equipment would be possible and whether such equipment could be stockpiled for distribution as necessary. Communications equipment in particular makes a vital contribution to the success of a peacekeeping operation and standardization both of such equipment and communications procedures would be desirable. Air transport is equally relevant to the success of United Nations missions.

Standby procedures and standardized load tables would be most useful. Military observers are usually available on fairly short notice from some countries, but as I have already emphasized, it is always helpful for the Secretary-General to be able to call upon as many governments as possible for assistance. Might it not be desirable, therefore, to outline the duties of a military observer and the kinds of abilities which a United Nations observer ought in theory to have?

Who is to make these studies? Some member states object to the Secretariat engaging in activities which it is said are the responsibility of the Military Staff Committee, that long neglected but still functioning body established by Article 47 of the Charter. As long as these objections are pressed the Secretariat would not seem to be able to do the job properly. What then about the Military Staff Committee? Its function, as outlined in the Charter, is to advise and assist the Security Council on all questions relating to the Council's requirements for the maintenance of international peace and security and the employment and command of forces placed at its disposal. It has failed to perform this function because after the war the Soviet Union was unable or unwilling to reach agreement with the other Permanent Members on the numbers and types of United Nations forces. At that time these forces were to be provided by the Permanent Members themselves and it was not surprising, given their very different experiences during the war, that they should find it impossible to agree on the contributions each should make to the United Nations.

The atmosphere of the cold war stifled any further work by the Military Staff Committee and its functions were afterwards executed by the Secretary-General. Now, however, the theory and practice of United Nations forces has changed. Their purpose has not been the enforcement of United Nations decisions against recalcitrant states but the supervision of agreed arrangements. The nonpermanent members have become the major troop contributors. A good deal of experience is available for analysis. There may be some basis for believing therefore that the Military Staff Committee, enlarged by the addition of several nonpermanent members as the Soviet Union has proposed, could work out some standard rules and regulations for peacekeeping.

Another possible answer to the question I have posed of who is to do the planning is that the governments chiefly concerned should do it themselves independently of the United Nations. This is a possibility which Canada explored in 1964 when we convened a conference of military experts from twenty-three governments to consider the technical aspects of United Nations peacekeeping. Since that time a somewhat similar conference has been held in Oslo. For our part, we are ready to carry further this process of informal consultation outside the strict framework of the United Nations whenever circumstances appear to warrant it. We are ready as well to produce guide books and training manuals based on our own experience, and after consultation with other governments concerned, to make them available for the use of the United Nations or of any of its members.

In considering the alternative ways of military planning that I have just described, Canada's principal concern will be the same now as in 1945; if we are to participate in United Nations police actions then we want to take part as well in the planning and decisions which will lead to those actions. An enlarged Military Staff Committee on which we would expect to be represented might be one convenient method of achieving these objectives. In any event, we are prepared to cooperate in whatever arrangements may be made, inside or outside the United

Nations, to improve the organization's capacity to fit its peacekeeping services to the diversity of present world conditions.

I want to take up now the second question I have asked: How are member states to share the responsibility of peacekeeping? This question raises what is, in my view, the central problem of peacekeeping: the procedures of political authorization and control. The primary purpose of the United Nations is to control conflict, by consent if possible, by enforcement action if necessary. The use of force or coercion is subject in principle to the agreement of the Permanent Members of the Council to its use. I say in principle because while it is clearly the sense of the Charter that coercive action cannot be taken by the United Nations without unanimous Great Power consent, it was also the expectation of the majority of governments at San Francisco that this consent would be forthcoming in cases of acts of aggression or flagrant breaches of the peace. When by 1950 this expectation had proved to be illusory, the Assembly asserted the right to make recommendations for the maintenance of peace and security, including the right to recommend the use of force to maintain or restore peace if there was a breach of the peace and the Council was prevented from taking appropriate action. Canada was a leading advocate of the Assembly's right to assert this residual power and has continued to be ever since, on the grounds that collective action to stop aggression is the overriding purpose of the organization and must not be frustrated by the abuse of the veto power.

We were confirmed in our opinion by the Assembly's role in the establishment of the United Nations Emergency Force in 1956. It has been argued that the recommendation to establish the Force was *ultra vires* of the Assembly's authority, because it was a military force with *potential* if not *actual* coercive functions. Whether or not the functions of the Force are defined as peacekeeping or enforcement action, and we have always thought it to be the former, seems to me to be irrelevant to the point that the Assembly can make recommendations for action in the circumstances I have described, and that such recommendations serve to implement the purposes of the United Nations if they obtain the required two-thirds majority.

The view is sometimes expressed that the expansion of the membership of the General Assembly has created a new situation and that peacekeeping operations might now be authorized which would ignore or defy the interests of important member states or even important groups of members. I think this is unlikely to happen because the Assembly is a political body, and in politics it is not customary to take actions which are self-defeating. A veto in the Council is one thing. Opposition to United Nations action by a number of powerful states is another. I think it very improbable that the Assembly would recommend a peacekeeping operation without making some provision for its financing and without knowing whether sufficient personnel and logistic support would be available.

On the other hand, I also think it might not be a bad idea if we were to take another look at the voting procedures of the Assembly. It is now possible to adopt important recommendations by a substantial majority which are quite unrelated to the facts of power in the world. Such recommendations remain "on the books," but they have little or no effect. This is not a procedure calculated to expand the influence of the Assembly or to enhance the prestige of the organization. The Foreign Minister of Ireland proposed two years ago that the Assembly change its rules of procedure in order to increase the number of affirmative votes required for Assembly recommendations on peace and security questions. I believe this proposal deserves careful study.

Whatever the rights and wrongs of this question, however, the fact remains that the argument reflects a deep split between the Permanent Members of the Council about how to exercise control over peacekeeping, and it has blocked any progress on financing and advance planning. As we all know such concepts as aggression or threats to peace have always been extraordinarily difficult to define to everyone's satisfaction. They are doubly so today, the era of such phenomena as wars of liberation, subversion and neocolonialism. Everywhere the status quo is under attack, often by violent means. The distinction between the internal and external affairs of states becomes blurred as does the very concept of the legitimacy of authority. The danger of great powers being drawn into local conflicts is increasing. It is understandable that these powers should wish to retain control over United Nations actions which are bound to affect their interests. It is difficult to agree, however, with the view of the Soviet Union that this control, includ-

ing the detailed supervision of peacekeeping operations, be exercised exclusively by the Security Council
and the Military Staff Committee. Even if there was a
moratorium on the use of the veto, could we reasonably expect a committee of this membership to run
peacekeeping operations without delay, disagreement,
or deadlock?

I do not think so. I believe the present system
whereby the Secretary-General directs peacekeeping
under the guidance of the Council is more in keeping
with today's blend of political and military realities.
No doubt this system might be improved. In particular the Military Staff Committee might be able to do
some useful advance planning, including the prep-
aration of a model agreement between the United
Nations and contributing governments. It might
possibly perform as well some advisory functions during the actual course of an operation. If this were to
be done its membership would need to include the
countries actually doing the peacekeeping at any one
time. Perhaps a compromise along these lines,
coupled with a tacit understanding not to pursue the
constitutional argument about the powers of the
Assembly, might enable us to get ahead. It is futile,
in any event, I believe, to insist on constitutional

positions which cannot be implemented in practice unless we are to rewrite the Charter. The fact is that interventions by the Assembly in the peacekeeping field have been exceptional. If the Permanent Members act responsibly it will not have cause to intervene again.

The aspects of peacekeeping I have been discussing relate by and large to Canada's view of the world from the gallery of the middle powers. But I would be guilty of distortion if I did not recall that Canada is also a Western country with a point of view which is shaped by her alliance commitments and responsibilities. United Nations efforts to keep the peace, I have suggested, are and will be successful insofar as they serve the interests of the principal groups of members and especially the Great Powers. They must tend therefore towards neutrality and passivity. The participants as well as the Secretary-General must hope that the balance of interests which brought about the intervention in the first place will generate the pressures that bring a peaceful political settlement. Canada of course will exert what influence she can to obtain such settlements. But, unlike the United Nations as an organization, we cannot always be impartial towards the issues themselves.

We must and do reserve the right to state our views on these issues in the framework of our foreign policy. If, in our judgment, the peacekeeping role in any particular case should not be consistent with our conception of a just or speedy settlement or with our national interests we would not hesitate to decline or to terminate Canadian participation. If we do participate, it is because in all the circumstances we believe it to be the most appropriate and most helpful action for us to take.

We have taken that action each time we have been asked to do so. Our general view has been that that United Nations is the most suitable international instrument to keep the peace. It may not be the best or most efficient. Regional organizations have a prior claim under the terms of the Charter itself, and the more disputes they can help to settle the less burdened will be the United Nations' agenda. Other disputes do not appear on the agenda because one or more of the parties are not United Nations members. The United Nations, however, is more likely to give a fair hearing to complaints and to provide a more generally acceptable procedure for saving face or gaining time. In Dag Hammarskjöld's words: "The greatest need today is to blunt the edges of conflict among the nations, not to sharpen them. If properly used, the United Nations can serve a diplomacy of reconciliation better than other instruments available to the member states." Canadians like to think that they serve themselves when they serve the United Nations.

✒ CANADA'S APPROACH
TO THE VIETNAM CONFLICT

IN MY FIRST lecture I dealt with the Canadian approach to peacekeeping by the United Nations and with ways in which the many obstacles to an effective exercise of this function might be overcome. For many reasons we believe that the United Nations, despite certain weaknesses, is, in the long run, the most suitable international instrument to keep the peace. For the present, we have to face the fact, however, that in certain situations the United Nations may be powerless to act and that other arrangements may have to be made to provide an international presence in sensitive areas.

The Geneva Conference of 1954, which brought an end to hostilities in Vietnam, Laos, and Cambodia, was the classic case of the attempt at peaceful resolution of conflict outside the United Nations

context. The conference on Indochina, which grew
out of the Berlin conference of the Big Four in January, 1954, and which was linked with the Korean
conference which preceded it, was limited in membership to the five Great Powers—the United States,
the Soviet Union, Communist China, Britain, and
France—and the four Indochina governments—Laos,
Cambodia, the State of Vietnam, and the Democratic
Republic of Vietnam. Five of the nine participants
were not at that time members of the United Nations, and the four permanent members of the Security Council who were involved in the Geneva Conference were as deeply divided on the issues of Korea
and Indochina as they were on the issues of Europe;
it is not surprising, therefore, that negotiations did
not take place under United Nations auspices.

The Geneva Conference achieved a cease-fire and
made an attempt at providing a basis for a long-term
political settlement in the area. It created, in the
International Commissions for Supervision and Control, a supervisory mechanism which to a large extent
ensured the short-term viability of the military cease-
fire arrangements. However, by not taking full account of the deep-rooted political and ideological
divisions which were never far beneath the surface,

the conference left unresolved certain issues which were fundamental to Indochina. As these issues emerged in new forms in the years following 1954 it became clear that, as in the United Nations, the absence of agreement among the big powers on long-term objectives, and irreconcilable contradictions among the countries directly involved, can undermine the effectiveness of any international peace-keeping operation.

I would like to examine the special case of Vietnam in some detail, not only because of the broad international implications of the war in Vietnam but also because Vietnam in many ways represents the severest test to which international peacekeeping has been put. There are many strands woven into the complex fabric of the Vietnam tragedy. As the Minister responsible for Canadian foreign policy, I shall examine the problem of Vietnam and peacekeeping from the point of view of Canada as a member of the International Supervisory Commissions. The Canadian decision to accept the invitation to participate in the International Commissions in Vietnam, Laos, and Cambodia represented the beginnings of a major Canadian involvement in Asia. Furthermore, nearly thirteen years of participation in international supervision in the area has inevitably led the Canadian Government to concentrate today on ways of achieving not only a peaceful settlement of the war but also a settlement which may be more permanent than the one attempted in 1954. Our experience has, of course, conditioned our point of view; on the other hand, this should not be interpreted as indicating any insensitivity to other viewpoints, and particularly to the wide range of considerations affecting the policy of the United States in the area.

During the postwar era Canada has played many roles in the world. It has been a loyal member of NATO throughout the many crises which have been faced in Europe; it was a member of the United Nations forces in the Korean war; it has been a participant in nearly every peacekeeping operation undertaken by the United Nations. In a sense, our role in Vietnam has been the most frustrating and disillusioning. Like many other countries, we have sensed a tragic inevitability in the developments leading up to the present war; as a member of the International Commission, with a direct responsibility for assisting in the maintenance of the peace in Vietnam, we have been particularly sensitive to the apparent inability of the countries involved in the area to deflect developments. As a result, we examine our own experience in an attempt to determine why the 1954 settlement went wrong, and how, when a new settlement is achieved, the same mistakes can be avoided.

The Vietnam crisis cannot, of course, be explained or understood solely in terms of the events of the past decade or two. As with so many of the states of the world which are struggling to modernize their political and economic structures, the problems of Vietnam are the problems of history, of political traditions, and of centuries of rivalry and war. The present division of Vietnam is not a new situation; the fact that a wall separated two warring dynasties in the seventeenth and eighteenth centuries is not irrelevant to any analysis of today's problems. The isolation of the villages of South Vietnam from central authority is not a modern phenomenon, but simply a continuation of a problem which even the most illustrious and powerful emperors of Vietnam were seldom able to resolve. The economic impoverishment of the area is acute when compared to the rising expectations of the modern age, but nevertheless is simply a continuation of an economic condition which has prevailed for hundreds of years. The effect on Vietnam's neighbors of the present political and military hostilities is little different from the clash of empires and the reactions to the steady territorial expansion of the Vietnamese people since the Middle Ages. Nevertheless, although it is necessary to recognize the continuity of these problems, the world of the mid-twentieth century is no longer prepared to accept their inevitability. The world community, in the nuclear age, is becoming increasingly conscious of the need to create an international order in which necessary political and social changes can be accomplished by peaceful means, and disputes between nations and peoples can be settled without violence. The resources of the developed world are being used more and more to break the chains binding the peoples of Asia to the poverty and violence of the centuries. The war in Vietnam presents a serious obstacle to these massive efforts, and if the historical roots of discontent and insecurity in Southeast Asia are to be effectively removed, a way must be found not only to bring that war to an end but also to provide a basis for a more viable settlement than the one projected by the Geneva Conference in 1954 turned out to be.

When the Geneva powers met in 1954, the war in Vietnam had been in progress for eight years and had spilled over into Laos and Cambodia. It was not, as is sometimes stated, a war between France on the one side and all Vietnamese nationalists, led by the Communists, on the other. In the beginning, France certainly played the role of a colonialist power attempting to maintain some kind of presence in the states of Indochina, and the Communist-led Vietminh were strongly motivated by nationalist feelings. Before long, however, subtle changes occurred. Nationalist non-Communist elements within the Vietminh were gradually denuded of power and influence or completely eliminated. The French at the same time found themselves allied with many Vietnamese who were just as determined as the Vietminh to achieve an independent Vietnam, but who were prepared to pursue their objective by political, rather than military, means and who were at least as opposed to Communist control as to French colonialism. As the war progressed, the differences between Vietnamese became more pronounced and there emerged, as there had before so often in Vietnamese history, two Vietnamese communities struggling for the right and the power to govern all of Vietnam.

When the élites reflecting these two communities went to Geneva in 1954, "North Vietnam" and "South Vietnam" did not exist. There were only two governments—one Communist and one non-Communist—both claiming sovereignty over the whole of Vietnam and over all Vietnamese. The Democratic Republic of Vietnam, recognized by all the countries of the Communist bloc, and the State of Vietnam, recognized by more than thirty other countries, both attended the Geneva Conference as sovereign states and as full participants in the deliberations of the conference, and the armed forces of both governments were intermingled in combat from the Chinese border in the north to the Camau Peninsula in the south. The State of Vietnam had, however, delegated command over its armed forces to the High Command of the French Union Forces, which had the primary responsibility for the conduct of the war, and it was perhaps only natural, therefore, that the burden of negotiations on the Franco-Vietnamese side should have been borne by France, especially in a conference dominated by the big powers. A sharp divergence of policy developed, however, between France, which intended to withdraw from Indochina, and the State of Vietnam, which intended to exercise its right to govern Vietnam. The State of Vietnam, from the beginning of the conference, had opposed the partitioning of the country and had pressed for United Nations supervision until peace and order could be restored, at which time free nationwide elections could be held under United Nations supervision. On the other hand, in the atmosphere of urgency which surrounded the conference, it was perhaps inevitable that the effective decisions concerning cease-fire arrangements should be negotiated by those in effective control of the armed forces engaged in the war, and that the position of the State of Vietnam concerning partition should have received so little attention during the efforts being made to separate and regroup the forces of both sides as quickly and as expeditiously as possible.

If this had been restricted to the cease-fire agreement which was ultimately signed by representatives of the French Union Forces and the Communist "People's Army of Vietnam," the implications probably would not have been serious. Arrangements, however, were also considered for the final political settlement, which envisaged general elections being held within two years to bring about the unification of Vietnam, even though no agreements were signed to this effect, and although the State of Vietnam explicitly dissociated itself from the projected arrangements.

With the wisdom of hindsight, we can see how the dragon's teeth were sown. But in July, 1954, there was a general sigh of relief throughout the world. The war in Indochina, with all its attendant risks, was over. Attention turned to the immediate tasks of the cease-fire agreements and to the arrangements for carrying them out. It was apparent that in the tense international atmosphere of the time, and in the wake of a bitter war, the peacekeeping role of the International Commissions would be vital.

Canada, although it had been represented at the Korean Conference, had not played any direct part in the negotiations on Indochina. The government was aware that the composition of the International Supervisory Commissions had been one of the important points of disagreement between the Communist and Western delegations, but it had no reason to anticipate the invitation which was extended to India, Poland, and Canada after the cease-fire agreements had been negotiated and signed. Acceptance of the invitation was not an easy decision. Canada was geographically remote from Indochina and had no traditional interests in the area. The settlement had been reached outside the United Nations, and that organization would not be involved in the supervisory function. Canada had not had a voice in creating the terms of reference under which it was now being asked to operate. Finally, we were very aware of the deep crosscurrents surrounding the Geneva Conference and recognized that the International Commissions themselves might be caught in the middle of any breakdown of the settlement.

Nevertheless, despite our reservations, and despite our recognition of the responsibilities and difficulties which membership in the Commissions would entail, Canada accepted the invitation. Canadian foreign policy was firmly committed to the peaceful resolution of disputes, and it was clear that the effectiveness of the cease-fire reached in Geneva would to some extent depend on the supervisory arrangements. It was true that the United Nations was not involved, but at least an international presence had been provided for: It was possible to hope that this presence might place some restraints on the big powers whose interests were so directly engaged in Indochina, and that the Commissions would exert a general stabilizing influence on the region.

It was clear that the Commissions would have only limited powers and resources; on the other hand, they had no responsibility themselves for the execution or enforcement of the agreements. The parties themselves were required to carry out their undertakings and if violations of the cease-fire agreements occurred, and if the recommendations of the Commissions were not implemented, the Commissions were expected to report the circumstances to the members of the Geneva Conference. Thus, although in the last analysis the fulfilment of the provisions of the cease-fire agreements in Vietnam, Laos, and Cambodia would depend on the cooperation of the parties, the Commissions, by acting as the eyes and ears of the international community, could perform a worthwhile function by providing an element of disinterested deterrence to open violations of the cease-fire.

Canada's decision in 1954 to participate in the Vietnam Commission represented an attempt to contribute to the peace and stability of Southeast Asia. It was clear that in proposing India, Poland, and Canada as members of the Commissions, Communist China had envisaged a *troika* arrangement in which Poland would represent the interests of one of the parties, Canada would represent the interests of the other, and India, as the major neutral power of the time, would cast the deciding votes. We were aware of the difficulties of the so-called "Neutral

Nations Commission" in Korea, in which the requirement for unanimity had hamstrung the Commission. The Indochina Commissions at least provided for majority decisions on a wide range of matters, and for majority and minority reports on the major issues.

Despite the temptation to live up to the conference's expectations, Canada decided from the beginning to avoid the role of rigid advocate for the West and, instead, tried to promote an objective and balanced approach by the Commissions. We were firmly convinced, and remain so to this day, that neither the work of the Indochina Commissions nor the future of international peacekeeping would be served if the members of the Commissions gave the impression of being swayed by political bias, and of ignoring the terms and intent of the cease-fire agreements in the interests of one side or another. We encountered many difficulties in carrying out this policy, but after thirteen years we remain convinced that it was the right one.

Because the 1954 settlement did not produce a lasting peace, it is sometimes argued that the International Commission in Vietnam failed in its role. As I have pointed out, however, the Commission was not envisaged as an enforcement agency: It had not been given the terms of reference, the authority, or the resources to impose its will on the parties, and was expected to leave the actual task of keeping the peace to those directly involved, to act in such a way as to encourage observance of the Cease-Fire Agreement, and to keep the members of the 1954 conference informed of results. The deterioration of the situation in Vietnam had complex origins, and although the weaknesses of the supervisory process no doubt contributed to the eventual breakdown, there were other important factors arising out of the nature of the 1954 settlement itself, the policies and objectives of the two Vietnams, and the atmosphere created by the policies of the major world powers.

Let us first of all look at the 1954 settlement. I have already mentioned how the anxiety of most of the major powers to achieve a cease-fire led to a situation in which little weight was given to the clearly stated position of the State of Vietnam. The conference, by ignoring the position of the government which claimed to speak for the non-Communist community of Vietnamese, and by projecting nationwide free elections in 1956, had set forth an objective which was certain to pose problems—unless of course the

State of Vietnam collapsed in the interim. The political objectives of the governments representing the two communities of Vietnam were in direct conflict, and this became more and more evident in the months following July, 1954. Furthermore, the government of the State of Vietnam, instead of collapsing, as many observers of the time expected it to do, consolidated its position and, by so doing, achieved the ability to resist in practice the political settlement which it had opposed throughout the Geneva Conference.

The political environment in Vietnam, therefore, was inherently unstable. The mandate of the International Commission, however, related not to the political settlement but to the supervision of the Cease-Fire Agreement. The history of the Commission's work in this field is fairly clearly set out in the various reports it submitted to the cochairmen of the Geneva Conference between 1954 and 1965. In summary, I think it is fair to say that the Commission was reasonably successful in its task of supervising and facilitating the disengagement of forces, and their regroupment in the two zones of Vietnam. Both the French High Command and the People's Army of Vietnam had an interest in implementing the cease-fire provisions, and as a result the Commission was able to act effectively and constructively during the early stages. On the other hand, when the interests of the two sides diverged, and when the Commission tried to supervise effectively aspects of the Cease-Fire Agreement which one side or the other felt interfered with its national objectives, the International Commission found its supervision interfered with, evaded or thwarted.

The agreement, for example, provided that in both zones the democratic freedoms of the population were to be guaranteed and that no reprisals were to be taken against persons for their activities during the hostilities. North Vietnam submitted innumerable complaints to the Commission alleging reprisals against persons in South Vietnam who were "former resistance workers." The South Vietnamese Government complained that North Vietnam was carrying out subversive activities in the south, and that the Commission would not be permitted to investigate allegations of reprisals until it took some action against North Vietnam for the alleged subversion. In neither North nor South Vietnam was the Commission ever able to ensure that "democratic freedoms" were extended to the populations. Similarly, despite the build-up of the North Vietnamese army in the period immediately following the cease-fire, the Commission was never able to detect the entry of a single piece of military equipment into the country. Violations of the Cease-Fire Agreement occurred in both North and South Vietnam and, although the Commission could from time to time report to the members of the Geneva Conference on at least some of these violations, there was no way in which pressure could be effectively brought to bear on the governments concerned to force them to remedy the situation. Indeed, because the Commission was dependent on services and facilities extended to it by the governments concerned, it was severely handicapped even in its attempts to investigate possible violations.

I have already referred to the *troika* structure of the Commission, which was designed to reflect what were assumed to be the three main blocs—Communist, Western, and "neutralist." Our experience since 1954 has not led us to believe that this type of control mechanism is well suited to international peacekeeping. If the assumption is made that two of the three members of the *troika* will automatically assume the role of advocate for their respective "sides," it is obvious that an intolerable burden will be placed on the third member, which is cast in the role of an arbiter. In effect, that third member is expected to assume the full responsibility for every decision which is taken by the peacekeeping agency and to accept, as a result, the foreign policy implications of such decisions as they apply to the arbiter itself. In a situation such as exists in Vietnam where, as I have said, Canada has consistently attempted to act objectively and to support findings against either side if they are substantiated by impartial investigation, the burden on the third country is reduced to some extent, but not, unfortunately, to the point where it can act without any reference at all to the implications for its own national position. We have encountered difficulties in our position too. I think it is generally assumed that Canada was named to the International Commission to represent Western interests. If this were understood and accepted by all parties, it would be possible, in theory at least, to act accordingly. Indeed, it would simplify the task. On the other hand, given Canada's role as a major participant in United Nations peacekeeping operations, it is impossible for us, in a situation such as Vietnam, to play the role of a special pleader for any one party without cutting across our broader goal of strengthening the United Nations as an impartial and objective agency for the settlement of international disputes.

I have touched on the contribution to the failure in Vietnam which was made by the 1954 settlement itself and by the weaknesses of the supervisory agency. There were, in addition, broader international factors which contributed to the deterioration of the situation. In 1954 the cold war between Communism and the West still existed in Europe, and only one year after the cease-fire had been achieved in the bitter Korean war an atmosphere of hostility permeated Asia. In this environment it was probably inevitable that in Vietnam—as in Germany, China, and Korea —the two communities should become the protégés of the major powers representing the ideological, political, and military division of the world at that time. The conflicting objectives of the two Vietnamese communities thus became the objectives of the Soviet Union and China on the one hand, and of the United States and other Western and Asian countries on the other. The line at the 17th parallel, which had created North and South Vietnam in 1954, had not been envisaged as a permanent frontier any more than had the lines between the two Berlins, the two Germanys, or the two Koreas. Nevertheless, the commitment of the prestige of the major powers to the protection of the two Vietnamese states made unification of the country impossible, and made the 17th parallel as sensitive a dividing line as the others.

The story of the succeeding years was best summed up by a majority report of the International Commission issued in mid-1962. The Commission, following examination and investigation of South Vietnamese complaints going back to 1955, informed the Foreign Ministers of Britain and the Soviet Union, acting as cochairmen of the Geneva Conference of 1954, that "armed and unarmed personnel, arms, munitions and other supplies" had been sent from North Vietnam into South Vietnam "with the object of supporting, organizing and carrying out hostile activities, including armed attacks directed against the armed forces and administration" of South Vietnam, and that the North Vietnamese authorities had allowed North Vietnamese territory to be used "for inciting, encouraging and supporting hostile activities in the zone in the South aimed at the overthrow of the administration" in South Vietnam. The Commission also reported that South Vietnam had received military aid from the United States in quantities in excess of those permitted by the Geneva Agreement of 1954 and had made military arrangements with the United States which amounted to a factual military alliance. The Commission recommended that all violations of the Cease-Fire Agreement should cease in order to avert the threat of the resumption of open hostilities. The recommendations of the Commission were not heeded: North Vietnam's campaign of infiltration and subversion increased, as did the entry of United States military personnel and equipment; and by the beginning of 1965, with the commitment of United States combat troops to the support of South Vietnam, the war had passed into a form not very different from that preceding the cease-fire in 1954. It continues to intensify.

With its special message of 1962, to which I have just referred, the International Commission passed into a new stage of its existence. We had to face the fact that the 1954 settlement had broken down completely and that a new war in Vietnam was confronting the international community. North Vietnam, which had signed the Cease-Fire Agreement, had, according to the evidence of the International Commission, violated the cease-fire in an attempt to establish the control over all of Vietnam which it had expected to achieve through the elections envisaged in the Final Declaration. South Vietnam, which did not consider itself bound by an agreement that it had not signed (but which had undertaken not to use force to resist the implementation of the cease-fire clauses), had also violated the cease-fire provisions. Progressively, the Cease-Fire Agreement had been eroded to a point where the International Commission remained its only functioning component.

The Canadian Government, although it recognized the futility of supervising a Cease-Fire Agreement which was being breached by both Vietnamese governments, considered that every effort had to be made to bring about an end of the war. We saw in the International Commission a symbol of the 1954 settlement, a possible channel for negotiations between the opposing forces in Vietnam, and the possible nucleus of some future settlement. Questions are sometimes raised in Canada about the desirability of continuing Canadian participation in the Commission. We have weighed the various aspects of the problem very carefully and we continue to believe that we should maintain our participation.

None of the interested parties has suggested that the International Commission should be withdrawn or that its mandate be cancelled. Furthermore, the Commission stands as a symbol of the 1954 Cease-Fire Agreement and can be considered as an indication of the continuing interest of the Geneva powers in the situation. Most important of all is our belief that in the right circumstances the Commission might be able to make a positive contribution to a peaceful settlement of the Vietnam issue. The Canadian Government has attempted on a number of occasions to explore, with its Commission colleagues India and Poland, the possibility that the Commission might play a useful role in bringing the opposing parties closer together. So far it has not been possible to achieve this objective. Nevertheless, we recognize that Canadian participation in the Commission provides us with a special opportunity to maintain a dialogue with the parties most directly involved in the war. Mr. Chester Ronning, the former Canadian High Commissioner to India, has made two visits to Hanoi as a special representative of the Canadian Government, and his visits were of great assistance in interpreting and clarifying the position of the North Vietnamese Government. The Canadian

Commissioner to the Vietnam Commission visits Hanoi frequently, and is able to have full and frank exchanges with the authorities there. During my visit to Europe last autumn I explored the problem in depth with the governments of Poland and the Soviet Union. I have maintained continuing consultation with all parties and personalities who are in a position to bring their influence to bear on behalf of peace in Vietnam. Canada has, of course, fully supported the constructive initiatives which have been taken by other nations of the world.

The fact that our efforts to contribute to the search for a peaceful settlement in Vietnam have not borne fruit is not, in my opinion, a reason for abandoning them. The present conflict must be brought to an end; a key must be found to open the door to an honorable negotiated settlement. We shall continue in our efforts to find that key.

Many attempts have been made to create circumstances in which talks or negotiations leading to a cease-fire, and opening the way to a lasting settlement, might begin. None of these attempts have succeeded, but they have made it possible to assess in some detail the positions of the two sides and to delineate fairly precisely the action required to roll back the level of hostilities to a point where discussion becomes possible. I recently suggested that the 1954 Cease-Fire Agreement, which concentrated on arrangements for a cease-fire and a disengagement of forces, contained the objectives which we are seeking today. It seems clear that, in existing circumstances, an overnight cease-fire cannot be expected. On the other hand, a progressive reapplication of the 1954 cease-fire terms would not only help to create a favorable climate for discussions between the two sides but, by enabling the two sides to engage in a step-by-step de-escalation, would itself create a certain momentum in the movement towards negotiations.

I would envisage the process being carried out in four stages. The first step would involve restoring the demilitarized character of the zone on either side of the 17th parallel and a reactivation of those provisions of the Cease-Fire Agreement which prohibit the use of either North or South Vietnam for the carrying out of hostile acts against the other. In my view, this step would have to include the bombing and any other military action against North Vietnam. The second stage would involve freezing the course of military events in Vietnam at its existing level. Both sides would undertake not to engage in any military activities which differed in either scale or pattern from existing activities; it might also involve a prohibition on the reinforcement of military personnel and equipment into North or South Vietnam from any source. The third stage would involve the cessation of all active hostilities between the parties. The fourth and final stage, which would complete the process of return to the cease-fire provisions of the 1954 settlement, would provide for the exchange of prisoners, the withdrawal of outside forces and the disposal of military bases.

I recognize, of course, that proposals such as this cannot contribute much to the situation until both sides are prepared to accept them. I remain convinced, however, that some process such as the one I have outlined must ultimately be accepted if we are to emerge from the Vietnam impasse.

It would be a mistake, however, to think that the commencement of talks and the opening of negotiations would automatically solve the problem of Vietnam. We have to bear in mind the lessons of the 1954 Conference and avoid any tendency to ignore the harsh political realities of the situation. We know now that these realities inevitably surface in a more virulent form unless appropriate arrangements are made to take them into account.

At this stage, it is of course impossible to set out a detailed formula for a lasting settlement in Vietnam and the neighboring area. Nevertheless, we think it is possible, on the basis of past experience and present facts, to set out certain broad considerations which will have to be taken into account if any settlement is to be more than simply a pause in a steadily deteriorating situation.

First, the fact that a military solution alone is neither practicable nor desirable has become almost a truism. It is becoming clear that in existing circumstances North Vietnam will not be able to impose its control over South Vietnam by military means or, more accurately, by the politico-military means which are the hallmark of "wars of national liberation." Given a stabilization of the military balance, the two regimes and the two communities in Vietnam will have to find ways of accommodating their respective interests and avoiding recourse to the violent methods which have led to the present war.

Second, some way will have to be found to return to the basic provisions of the Geneva Cease-Fire

Agreement of 1954. In practice, this will of course involve a continuation of the *de facto* division of Vietnam—a situation which neither North nor South will view with equanimity. Nevertheless, it seems evident that until ways can be found to blur and ultimately eliminate the dividing line by peaceful means, and by mutual consent, the alternative is a continuation of the present dangerous situation.

Third, we must recognize that although a return to the 1954 cease-fire arrangements holds out the best hope for a beginning of a lasting settlement, the people of Vietnam are one people and must ultimately join together in one country. For the time being, however, the participants in a future conference must face up to the fact that there are two distinct communities in Vietnam, just as there are two communities in Korea and in Germany, and that these two communities must both agree when and how arrangements should be made for reunification. Most of the big powers at the 1954 Geneva Conference paid lip service to the cause of reunification, but in the circumstances of the time were led to ignore the existence of the two communities; we have seen the tragic results of this mistake. We see no reason, however, why the realities of the situation should lie too heavily on the individuals affected, and we would hope some arrangement could be worked out whereby reasonably free movement between the two zones could be permitted to allow at least the reunification of families.

Fourth, we think it inevitable that any settlement in Vietnam will have to be effectively supervised by an international presence. We would expect all outside forces to withdraw from both parts of Vietnam as soon as conditions permitted, and we would hope that both Vietnams would undertake to avoid inflammatory propaganda attacks on each other in the interests of contributing to the development of the kind of atmosphere that will make possible meaningful contacts between them. Whatever the terms of a settlement, however, both Vietnams and the other countries directly involved will want assurances that the terms of the settlement are being carried out. I would expect that international supervision, to be successful, would have to be backed up by firm understandings between the major powers involved in the settlement and by some form of guarantees by these same powers.

Fifth, although we have no firm views as to what form international supervision might take, we think it will be generally accepted that the international agency involved should be so constituted as to have the confidence of all parties to the settlement. As I have mentioned, the present Commission has a number of weaknesses, and it may be necessary to give a new agency a different composition, more clearly defined and more effective powers, and greater resources; otherwise, there will always be the risk that the parties directly concerned with the problem will consider it necessary to resort to unilateral action to rectify breaches of agreements. This, as we know, could mean the complete breakdown of the settlement. As far as Canada is concerned, I would be prepared to recommend that we cooperate, within the limits of our available resources, in the constitution of a new supervisory force. We would also expect to contribute, on the basis of our long experience in the area, our judgment and our advice on the nature of the supervisory agency.

Sixth, we believe that the Vietnamese people, like all peoples of the world, should be able to determine their own political future and create their own institutions. We have welcomed the progress which has been made in South Vietnam to bring about the conditions in which a constitutional government, responsive to the wishes of the people, can be elected. We would anticipate that, with the creation of a peaceful environment, ways could be found to provide an opportunity for all segments of the South Vietnamese population—including adherents of the Vietcong—to participate in the political life of South Vietnam on the same basis as other groups. I would like to hope that the same opportunities could be extended to the population of North Vietnam. The creation of constitutional and responsive governments in both parts of Vietnam would, I am convinced, contribute much to a peaceful resolution of differences. There is no doubt in my mind that the populations of both Vietnams are anxious to find peaceful ways of coming together and to avoid a recurrence of the present situation.

There are, of course, other issues lying beyond Vietnam which must be resolved if peace is to be achieved and maintained in that country. Laos and Cambodia, who both aspire to a neutral status which would protect them against outside interference, must be given an opportunity to pursue their own destinies. In 1962 an agreement guaranteeing the neutrality of Laos was negotiated and signed by fourteen countries. Despite this, the International Commission has reported major violations of the settlement by North Vietnam and is awaiting permission to enter Communist-held areas in order to investigate charges of United States violations. I think there is much merit in proposals which have been made for the neutralization of Vietnam and much of the rest of Southeast Asia, and I would think most of the countries of the region would wish to acquire neutral status if this could be effectively guaranteed and if it would prevent the constant interference in their internal affairs which is so prevalent today.

In the background, of course, is the great question of Communist China, without whose cooperation no lasting stability can be achieved in Vietnam or any other part of Southeast Asia. To some extent, the policies of China can be interpreted as the result of fear, insecurity, and wounded pride. It is difficult, I know, to find a prescription which will eliminate these deeply rooted elements of Chinese policy; on the other hand, I am convinced that it is in all our interests to continue our attempts to penetrate the wall of suspicion and hostility which surrounds the leaders in Peking.

Finally, we recognize the close links which exist between the requirements of stability in Southeast

Asia and the requirements of economic development. The United States has already made an immense contribution to these requirements and has promised even greater commitments once peace is established. Canada, through the Colombo Plan, its participation in the Mekong Basin project, and through its commitments to the Asian Development Bank, is also playing its role in this area and we shall continue to do so.

The task of bringing permanent peace and stability to Vietnam and Southeast Asia is an immense one, which I am sure will occupy not only the countries of that region but the whole world community for many years to come. Any formula for peace will inevitably be as complex as the factors involved in the present situation, and the path to a right formula will be strewn with obstacles and disappointments. Nevertheless, the war in Vietnam must be brought to an end, and the peaceful future not only of Vietnam but all of Southeast Asia must be assured. Since 1954 Canada has done its best to prevent a war in Vietnam. It is now doing its utmost to help to bring the war to an end. When a settlement is achieved, we shall do our best to ensure that it is a permanent one.

CANADA'S CONTRIBUTION TO
ECONOMIC DEVELOPMENT IN THE
LESS DEVELOPED WORLD

IN MY FIRST lecture in this series, I attempted to show how Canada's policies in support of United Nations peacekeeping activities reflected the Canadian outlook on the world. In my second lecture, I discussed in some detail the position which Canada has adopted towards the most potentially dangerous, violent conflict in the world today, the war in Vietnam. For this third and last lecture, I am turning to a different aspect of the search for world peace: the task of international development and Canada's distinctive contribution to it.

It is certainly an oversimplification to see in international development a means of eliminating all threats to peace. The principal antagonists in the two great wars of this century were and are among the most economically advanced countries of the world; this provides convincing and tragic proof that the hunger for power cannot be satisfied by material well-being alone. But in this latter half of the twentieth century, it has become increasingly clear that a world community which is half rich and half poor cannot be stable or peaceful. His Holiness Pope Paul VI expressed this fact in a profound yet simple way, when he said that "development is the new name for peace."

With the benefit of historical perspective, we can see that the origins of the present disparity in wealth among the world's peoples lie in the pattern of European economic and colonial expansion which took place in the eighteenth and nineteenth centuries. It was in Europe that the technological innovations which provided the key to our present-day economic prosperity in the Western world were first developed and applied. The resulting trade patterns, related as they were to the building of worldwide European empires, left the world with a set of economic relationships manifestly unsuited to the aspirations and needs of a world which has come to recognize the dignity and right to equal opportunity of all peoples.

Canada, like the United States, is itself a product of European colonial expansion. As a country of

European settlement, however, our peoples brought
with them the skills and aptitudes, and the psycho-
logical makeup, which enabled them to share from an
early stage the rapid technological and economic
development which had begun in Europe. But the
effort to build a new nation in North America has
also, I think, given us some insight into the problems
facing those nations in other parts of the world which
have recently attained independence, and have simultaneously embarked with determination on the
path of economic and technological development.

In earlier days, the needs of other countries for
outside assistance in achieving economic development would have gone largely unnoticed and un-
heeded. Indeed, it is only in relatively recent times
that the concept of collective, governmental action to
provide basic social services and stimulate economic
development within our own borders has been recognized. From an historical point of view, we may regard the Second World War as the turning point,
which led to the realization, still unfortunately not
fully accepted in all quarters, that responsibility for
human welfare cannot be limited by political boundaries. During the War, thousands of Canadians fought
and died, not only for the freedom of their own coun-

try, but also for the freedom of our allies, and for the beliefs which we shared with them. It was only natural that the sense of common purpose which characterized our war effort should be expressed anew in the task of reconstruction, an essentially economic task which required the contribution of material resources from the countries which had suffered least to those which had suffered most.

Amidst the revolutionary changes which took place in the world in the years following 1945, it was borne home to us that the countries which had been devastated by war were not the only ones where people were suffering from poverty and deprivation. First the great nations of Asia, proud heirs to ancient civilizations, and then the peoples of Africa raised their voices, demanding the same freedom and independence that the victorious allies had fought for in the Second World War. Initially, this great revolutionary movement was expressed in essentially political terms, but it soon became clear that the quest for political independence was only the first stage in a much more basic search for a better and more fully satisfying life.

In 1950 Canada met with Britain, Australia, New Zealand, India, Pakistan, and Ceylon to discuss ways of meeting the political, economic, and social problems that faced the newly independent Commonwealth countries of south and Southeast Asia. The result was the Colombo Plan, originally conceived as a Commonwealth response to what was regarded as a Commonwealth responsibility. To Canadians, the "new" Commonwealth which emerged in the years following the War was a source of some pride, for it was Canada which had originally pioneered the pattern of national independence within the Commonwealth. Canada was anxious to do what it could to make this "new" Commonwealth, embracing non-European as well as European peoples, a viable concept, and accordingly undertook to assist in the joint development effort which was so clearly needed. It is from that time that we can trace the growth of Canada's program of aid to the developing countries.

For the eight years following its inception, the Colombo Plan was Canada's only bilateral aid program, and to it the Canadian parliament appropriated annually the sum of $25 million. Despite the addition of other areas of the world to the Canadian assistance effort, the Colombo Plan region continues to receive the bulk of Canadian aid funds. Between 1950 and March of this year, bilateral assistance provided to the area totalled $800 million, of which an overwhelming proportion went to India and Pakistan. In this respect, Canadian allocations followed proportionately similar lines to those of the United States, Britain, and West Germany. I am frequently asked by Canadians why such a large proportion of our funds are allocated to the Indian subcontinent. It is important to remember, when making comparisons of this nature, that India and Pakistan contain more people than the continents of Africa and Latin America put together. In the last fifteen years, aid to India from all sources and of all types has amounted to little more than $20 per person, but this low per capita figure nevertheless represents the staggering aggregate investment of nine billion dollars.

The character of our aid to India and Pakistan has been one of heavy emphasis on power infrastructure projects, which often benefit agriculture as well, plus an increasing amount of grant aid food. Our food aid program to India alone in 1966 was $75 million in grants, a contribution which moved us ahead of the United States as a supplier on a comparative basis either of population or gross national product. The needs of India continue to be immense, and sometimes, when we look at the gloomy picture drawn by statistics of increasing population and food supplies diminished by drought, we may be tempted to despair. We should not forget, however, that India has put together in the last fifteen years the important beginnings of a modern industrial structure, and has an expanded force of trained and educated manpower. Together with its potentially rich resources of land and water, India has a far better base for economic progress than existed fifteen years ago. Much the same can be said with respect to Pakistan.

I want to deal at a later stage with our multilateral relationships, but no discussion of Colombo Plan aid would be complete without a reference to the confidence we have in the future of the Asian Development Bank, at the inauguration of which, last year, Canada pledged an initial capital contribution of $25 million. From its resources, we hope, will come great undertakings similar in scope and imagination to the Mekong development project (sponsored by the Economic Commission for Asia and the Far East), which serves Thailand, Laos, Cambodia, and Vietnam, and which awaits only the resolution of the area's political differences to take a great step forward.

In 1958, Canada decided to broaden the scope of

its contribution to international development by undertaking a new program of assistance for the islands of the British West Indies. Canadians had long felt a special sense of attachment to the West Indies, based among other things on the traditional trade in saltfish from the Maritime Provinces for West Indian sugar and rum. The establishment in the West Indies of a federation embracing the various islands, and the prospect of this federation becoming a second independent Commonwealth nation in the Western Hemisphere, gave added impetus to Canadian interest in the region. Initially, Canada's economic assistance was concentrated on the provision of infrastructure which would make the Federation more viable, and took the form, among other things, of two cargo-passenger vessels for interisland service.

The collapse of the West Indies Federation in 1962 ended, at least for the moment, the dream of a single united Commonwealth nation in the Caribbean, but it did not end Canadian interest in assisting the various West Indian territories to overcome the problems of development which confront them. Indeed, with the attainment of independence by Jamaica and Trinidad and Tobago, and later by Guyana and Bar-

bados, Canadian interest in strengthening and giving
new meaning to its special relationship with the area
has intensified. This was the background for the
important conference held in Ottawa in July, 1966,
and attended by the Prime Minister and Chief Ministers of all the Commonwealth Caribbean countries,
at which various avenues of collaboration in achieving development were explored. At that Conference,
Canada made it clear that the Commonwealth Caribbean would be considered an area of concentration in
the Canadian aid program. Even before the Conference, the Commonwealth Caribbean was receiving
more assistance from Canada, on a per capita basis,
than any other part of the world.

Africa, a continent with which Canada had only
the most tenuous relationships in prewar years, was
the third area to come within the ambit of our aid
program. You will recall the great upsurge of independence which characterized the African scene in
the years following 1957. Many of the newly independent states had been British dependencies, and
became members of the Commonwealth; others were
formerly colonies of France and Belgium, and became heirs to the French language and culture. Thus

it is in Africa that expression can be given in our aid program to Canada's own dual heritage.

Canadian assistance to Africa began in 1960, with an allocation for the Commonwealth African countries. In 1961 this was followed by the inauguration of a program for the francophone countries. Throughout Africa the most immediate need was for educational and technical assistance, and it was in these fields that we originally concentrated most of our attention. Recently, however, increasing emphasis has been placed on the need for capital projects, particularly for preinvestment and feasibility surveys, to enable the countries of Africa to make better use of their rich natural resources. From modest beginnings, our programs for both Commonwealth and francophone Africa have grown rapidly, as we have gained a greater understanding of Africa's needs and how they can be effectively met.

We were heavily involved in Asia, had undertaken a significant program in the Commonwealth Caribbean, and faced a growing need in Africa, but could we afford to ignore the circumstances of Latin America? This was a difficult question. On the one hand, there was no doubt at all in our minds that the requirements of Latin America deserved the attention of the industrialized world. We had extensive diplomatic and commercial ties, and the sympathy that must come from our common membership in the American family. On the other hand, we lacked facility in the two major languages of the region, and we ran the risk of spreading our program too thinly among the developing areas of the world. The decision, taken in 1964, was to allocate $10 million from our newly-created development loan fund to Latin America for projects which would be submitted for our approval through the Inter-American Development Bank. The fund has grown by annual installments, and by the end of this year, we shall have made loans for several major development projects in a number of Central and South American countries.

In addition to our program of bilateral assistance, Canada has participated actively from the beginning in the great international institutions that have grown up around the United Nations, drawing their strength from its universal approach. In 1966, Canada ranked fourth among the contributors to the United Nations Development Programme and the International Development Association, third in contributions to the United Nations Relief and Works Agency, and second in contributions to the World Food Programme.

Above all, we value the association we have established with the World Bank, which has become the repository of so much invaluable information and knowledge about the science of development assistance. The Bank, and its offspring, the International Development Association, are playing a major role in international development. As a member of the World Bank consortia for India, Pakistan, and the Indus Basin Development Fund, and of the consultative groups for Colombia, Malaysia, Nigeria, Thailand, and Tunisia, we are convinced of the merit of this orderly approach to a nation's development requirements, and we look for the formation of more of these groups. We have been favorably impressed by the reports drawn up by the Bank, by the International Monetary Fund, and by the promise of more detailed planning conveyed by the terms of reference of the United Nations Development Programme, all of which help us to determine the most effective ways of allocating funds under our bilateral programs.

Like other countries which have undertaken programs of development assistance, Canada has found the Development Assistance Committee of the Organization for Economic Cooperation and Development particularly useful as a means of coordinating our common effort. The Development Assistance Committee was created in 1960, precisely to counter some of those old arguments about uncoordinated bilateral aid, and to provide a meeting place where donors could exchange confidences. The initial concern of the Development Assistance Committee was with the equitable sharing of the responsibility for providing assistance, and for this purpose it undertook to establish statistical measurements of the flow of resources to countries in the course of economic development.

The Development Assistance Committee, under its firstrate chairman, Mr. Willard Thorp, has performed its task well, both in the area of burden-sharing and statistical analysis, as well as in the stimulation of increased volume and the promotion of more reasonable terms of aid. I make no criticism of its past endeavors, however, when I say that a new impetus is required from this forum, in which most of the Western donors, Australia, and Japan are represented. The Development Assistance Committee has known, as have the World Bank and the United Nations, that our joint efforts are faltering. The encouraging increases in the expansion of aid that took place before 1961 have not been repeated, and the terms on which assistance is extended are hardening, building repayment problems for the future. It may well be time for the Development Assistance Committee to speak to its members a little more firmly, and to exercise the moral suasion its unique position commands.

We have the assurance of the World Bank that the developing countries could make effective use of at least another $4 to $5 billion annually than they are now receiving. This means that the Bank has judged the problems of disbursement and absorption as not insurmountable, and indicates an encouraging view of the possibility of speeding up the timetable of development. I do not know if this volume can be attained in the short run. Taking the practical view, I find it hard to believe that we can collectively achieve a 35 per cent increase in all forms of aid within, say, the next five years, but drawing upon the experience of war, I am not unconscious of the fact that amazing results can be obtained from singlemindedness of purpose.

But of equal importance, can we provide this aid

on terms which will be of long-term assistance to the developing world? It is a sobering fact that the developing countries pay out between them $3.5 billion a year for servicing their external public debt and twice that sum when private commitments are included. The poorest among them, a former World Bank official has estimated, are now repaying more in interest and principal on World Bank loans than they are receiving in disbursements from the Bank. If we increase the amount of capital available without considering the impact of our terms on the developing countries, we could be compounding current difficulties and postponing indefinitely the creation of conditions of self-sustaining economic growth.

In planning for Canada's program of development assistance, we have been deeply conscious of the need for more aid, and for aid on better terms. At the present time, Canadian aid in all forms amounts to approximately $300 million a year, which is about three-fifths of one per cent of our Gross National Product. In a period when the level of assistance to the developing countries has been tending to remain static, Canada has taken the decision to expand its contribution to international development to an amount approximately equal to one per cent of its Gross National Product by the early nineteen seventies.

The terms of Canadian aid have always been relatively favorable. In the beginning, almost all our aid was in the form of grants, and grant aid continues to make up a substantial proportion of our total allocations. When the level of aid was expanded and it was decided to make aid available in loan form, the terms were based on those offered by the International Development Association, that is, no interest, ten years' grace, and repayment over a further period of forty years. Last year, even the three-quarters of one per cent service charge on this type of assistance was eliminated. We recognized, however, that some developing countries could usefully handle loans with somewhat higher repayment obligations, and to meet this particular need a type of loan carrying interest at three per cent, with seven years' grace, and thirty years' maturity was introduced.

The third type of loan available, of course, is that issued under the terms of Canada's Export Credits Insurance Act. These are extended on a commercial basis but qualify as development assistance because their terms are softer than those which could be ex-

tended directly by Canadian exporters. We include
these loans in our aid program figures because they
form part of the internationally accepted measure of
flow, while accepting the argument that they are designed primarily to serve the Canadian exporter. At
one time, export credits represented almost one-third
of the entire program, but in the year just past they
accounted for only one-sixth, and the proportion is
expected to grow smaller each year.

Canada maintains the policy of insisting that its
aid be given in the form of Canadian goods and services, of tying our aid funds, in other words, to procurement in Canada. We do this of economic necessity, rather than by conviction, because our sympa-
thies lie with the terms of the recommendation
adopted by the Development Assistance Committee
in July, 1965, which said, in part:

[Tying of aid] can bring about cumbersome limitations on
the freedom of the recipient to choose freely the most
suitable sources of supply on the international market.
With regard to bilateral assistance, member countries
should jointly and individually endeavour, unless inhibited
by serious balance of payments problems, to reduce progressively the scope of aid tying with a view ultimately
to removing procurement restrictions to the maximum
amount possible.

A significant proportion of Canadian aid is channeled through the multilateral agencies and is, of course, already untied. In respect to our bilateral aid we are willing, indeed anxious, to move from our position in concert with our fellow donors, particularly those whose economic influence in the world is so much greater than that of Canada. To be realistic, I cannot visualize early international agreement on this question, considering the disparate nature of aid programs and donor economies. I am, however, hopeful that it will be possible to arrive at a formula which would permit gradual movement towards the objective.

In the meantime we have done our best to mitigate the possible adverse effects of tying aid. Procedures have been adopted to ensure that there will be competitive bidding by our exporters, and we make available a sufficiently broad range of goods and services to enable the recipient country to avoid those with a relative price disadvantage. Perhaps I may observe, at this time, that as the result of aid associations extending over a period of fifteen years, the kind of request made to us today is usually for the kind of service or material that we offer on a world-

wide competitive basis of price and quality. Another
step we have taken is to reduce the emphasis formerly
placed on financing only the foreign exchange component of a project. In the Caribbean area, in particular, we have indicated our willingness to assume a
proportion of local costs where this is necessary to
ensure the completion of a high priority project.

We have also recognized the need for what is
called program or nonproject aid. The very pace of
development exerts a pressure on such countries as
India and Pakistan to use more and more foreign exchange to feed the increasing demands of a growing
industrial economy. To meet this need for raw material and spare parts, we have developed a large-scale
commodity program, primarily for the larger Asian
countries, and have adopted procedures that enable
users to enter into direct relationships with Canadian suppliers.

From what I have already said, it will, I think, be
clear that Canada's programs of development assistance represent a significant contribution to the international effort to build a more peaceful and stable
world community, capable of meeting successfully
the problems of social change and economic development that characterize our times. Aid is, of course,

only one of the ways in which the developed countries can contribute to the process of international development. As a result of the work of the United Nations Conference on Trade and Development, we have begun to obtain a clearer understanding of the role which trade can and must play in this process. Unless the trading opportunities of the developing countries are significantly improved, it may well prove impossible for them ever to attain self-sustaining growth.

For many of the developing countries, the export of basic commodities accounts for a large proportion of total earnings from trade, and it is therefore a matter of urgency to stabilize and improve their earnings from these commodity exports. This can only be done effectively through international commodity agreements, and Canada has been participating actively in the negotiations which are taking place with respect to several commodities. There is need also to open up larger markets for the products of the industries which the developing countries are establishing. While understandably concerned about the possibility of market disruption, Canada has a relatively good record in providing a market for manufactured goods from the developing countries. We are very hopeful that the tariff negotiations currently being concluded in Geneva—the Kennedy Round—will result in a more rational and efficient international division of labour, and thus be of particular benefit to the developing countries, as well as to the international community in general.

Because of the increasing realization that trade relationships are of great importance in international development, and the failure of aid programs to have the full impact that had at one time been expected, there are those who argue that trade, not aid, is the real answer to the problem of underdevelopment. This is, I believe, an oversimplification of the issue, for the provision of capital assistance and manpower training under development assistance programs, and the provision of wider market opportunities for the products of the developing countries, are really two sides to the same coin of international development. With the experience gained over the past two decades, Canada, like the other countries which have undertaken programs of development assistance, has come to realize that the task of international development is much more complex, and more formidable, than was once thought. We have realized that a long-term effort will be required and, with specific reference to our aid programs, that more sophisticated and comprehensive administrative arrangements, and more clarity and precision with respect to objectives, will be necessary.

The purpose of aid, as we see it, is clearly and simply to help the less-developed countries of the world achieve a degree of economic development which accords with the needs and aspirations of their peoples. Unfortunately, this basic, central objective has all too often been obscured and distorted by conflicting considerations. If genuine international development is to take place on the scale desired, and with the necessarily limited resources available, it is essential that the goal of economic development be kept at the forefront of our thinking, and that other goals be discarded, or at least placed in a subordinate position.

There is, for example, a tendency in some quarters to regard aid as a means of exerting political influence. Given the conflict of ideologies which is such an important feature of the international scene, this tendency is perhaps understandable. Certainly, we would hope that the attainment of economic development will encourage the less developed countries to evolve systems of government consonant with our

own ideals of liberty, an open society, and respect for
the rule of law. It should be noted, too, that a certain
degree of confidence and understanding must exist
between donor and recipient governments, if only to
make possible the administrative arrangements necessary for the successful operation of an aid program.
But it is, I think, a grave error to view aid as a means
of gaining immediate political objectives, or of buy-
ing friends. Experience has clearly shown that such a
view may not only lead to disappointment, but can
result also in the waste of scarce resources and a failure to achieve any sort of meaningful economic result.

Another goal which is sometimes claimed for aid
programs, and which I think is also of doubtful va-
lidity, is the attainment of immediate commercial
benefit for the donor country. Economic progress in
the developing countries will in the long run result in
expanding trade opportunities on a global scale, but
aid programs which have as their principal purpose
the stimulation of production in the donor country
are not likely to be very relevant to the economic
needs of the less developed countries. The drive and
know-how of businessmen in our free enterprise economies must, of course, be utilized in the implementa-

tion of aid projects, but to confuse aid programs with the promotion of exports, in itself a perfectly legitimate and necessary field of government action, is to run the risk of failing to achieve the objectives of either.

There is also, I think, a risk involved in regarding aid as charity, or as some kind of massive international relief effort. Special emergency measures must, of course, be taken from time to time on an international scale for the relief of human suffering, and such measures often tend to find their way into aid programs. It would be morally and humanly wrong not to provide assistance when the alternatives are sickness, starvation, and death. But such measures, if they are allowed to become the foundation of an aid program, may well make it more difficult to achieve effective and lasting economic progress in the long run. Certainly a spirit of humanitarianism is an important motive for the provision of aid, but there is, I think, a danger that overemphasis on charitable and humanitarian motives may lead us to underestimate the need for sound policies and effective, practical administrative arrangements.

If the goal of economic development must be accorded the dominant position in the thinking of the developed countries with respect to aid programs, it is equally important that the developing countries themselves evolve policies clearly aimed at this goal. While shortage of investment capital and skilled manpower are two of the principal obstacles to development, and can be at least partially overcome through international development assistance programs, there are other obstacles which only the developing countries themselves are in a position to tackle effectively. One of these is, of course, the rapid rate of population growth which characterizes so many countries, and has reduced the effectiveness, in per capita terms, of so much of the development that has taken place in recent years. Another factor which may inhibit growth in some developing countries is small size, which of course results in a small market and loss of the advantages which may be gained from economies of scale. One response to this problem is regional economic, and perhaps even political, integration. It is encouraging to note that increasing numbers of developing countries are seriously examining the possibilities of integration and other forms of cooperation to achieve economies of scale.

In allocating their aid, donor countries are certainly obliged to look for some evidence of performance on the part of the recipients, but I think we must recognize at the same time that governments in the developing countries are no less free from day-to-day pressures than governments in developed countries, and are often less well-equipped to cope with them. As one commentator recently noted, a developing country is faced with the necessity of balancing orderly growth against the disorderly demands of the present. When we recall that almost all developing countries are simultaneously undergoing rapid social change, and are engaged in evolving their own national personalities, it is clear that the criteria which donor countries must apply to ensure effective use of the resources they are contributing need to be tempered by an understanding of, and sympathy for, the particular problems faced by individual developing countries.

Development is not a simple mechanical process, and does not take place in a vacuum; it is influenced and shaped by a great many factors, among the most important of which are those associated with the culture and traditions of the countries concerned. Statistics on economic growth, although important, are not the sole indication of a successful development effort, for a developing country can hardly be expected to pursue economic growth to the exclusion of other goals which it may regard as important, such as a balanced distribution of wealth, and respect for its cultural heritage.

What this means, of course, is that genuine development is an endogenous process; while it can be assisted from without, it must be produced from within. In the final analysis, the quest for development involves not only higher standards of material wellbeing, but also the sense of responsibility and self-reliance that can come only from the successful achievement of a common goal by means of one's own efforts. The role of aid is to make this task easier and less costly in terms of social and human values, but aid can never be more than a supplementary factor in the overall process of development. Unfortunately, aid may have a tendency to enhance the cultural influence of the developed countries within the developing world, at a time when the most profound problems of the developing countries involve the need to break with this influence, at least to some extent. To recognize this is not to question the value or necessity of aid programs; it is rather to point out some of the pitfalls, and to underline the need for true generosity of spirit, as well as generosity of purpose, in approaching the task of international development.

In this lecture, I have attempted to outline Canada's approach to international development, and how the form and direction which Canadian aid programs have taken reflect Canada's own makeup and economic capabilities, as well as its outlook on the world. To conclude both this lecture and the series, I can think of no more fitting words than those of Pope Paul VI in his recent encyclical, words which can, I believe, serve as an inspiration to us all:

Excessive economic, social and cultural inequalities among peoples arouse tensions and conflicts, and are a danger to peace. . . . To wage war on misery and to struggle against injustice is to promote, along with improved conditions, the human and spiritual progress of all men, and therefore the common good of humanity. Peace cannot be limited to a mere absence of war, the result of an ever-precarious balance of forces. No, peace is something that is built up day after day, in the pursuit of an order intended by God, which implies a more perfect form of justice among men.